OSKAR KOKOSCHKA

ANTHONY BOSMAN

Oskar Kokoschka

BLANDFORD PRESS

LONDON

editor: Anthony Bosman
translation: Albert J. Fransella
lay-out: Wim van Stek
first published in the English edition in 1964 by
Blandford Press Ltd, London
reproduction with permission of Roman Norbert Ketterer,
Campione d'Italia
© 1964 and printed in Holland by The Ysel Press Ltd, Deventer

OSKAR KOKOSCHKA

Some people consider it a disparagement of purely artistic values when the work of a painter is discussed not only in relation to his own personality, but also—and perhaps even more—in relation to the spiritual and socio-economic structure of the time, of which every form of art is a reflection.

There are, of course, individuals whose creative works appear to have sprung from an almost isolated and self-sufficient spirit. Even with such artists, where the work of art does not originate from the fruitful interaction between the "I" and the "we" but is the result of an endless dialogue between the conscious and the subconscious ego, there is always evidence, difficult though it may be to recognize, of a constant relationship, positive or negative, with the basic realities of the age.

Appreciation of the values of pictorial art is not relegated to the background by psychological analysis. Paintings can, just as pictures, enthrall the spectator, but they still have a spiritual content. In isolation they lose everything save their aesthetic quality; when the aesthetic and the spiritual are united they express the very soul of the painter.

Particularly in the case of Oskar Kokoschka, it is impossible to separate his work, his personality and his period. The work of this artist is part and parcel of the cultural, political and social world in which he lives, thinks and works. With his deep interest in education, his active struggle for democracy, his writings, his plays and his strong inclination towards symbolism, he has given clearer evidence than many others of his aims and of his attitude towards the many problems which have come to the fore since the First World War. In everything he has done we find the man Kokoschka fully expressed—a man who lives passionately and enjoys the blessing of vision but who, even in his most enraptured moments, does not lose his capacity for sharp perception and is always in close contact with reality.

In this respect he is one of the very rare figures of our time, for there are very few painters for whom, personally, art means more than the gift of being able to express themselves pictorially as completely as possible. With Kokoschka, however, art is an active participation in the world, in its joys and its sorrows, sometimes emphatically in symbolic paintings, often in purely pictorial, non-symbolic pictures, and this certainly implies a spiritual condition which attains visionary stature.

His portraits are not merely portraits, nor are his landscapes just landscapes or his animal pictures just pictures of animals. There is much more in each of them. The portraits are soundings of psychic tensions, the landscapes are living organisms, the animal pictures are illustrations of elementary passions, of conflict and yet, also, of the harmony of nature.

It is this "more" that gives the art of Kokoschka a significance that raises it far above European expressionism. It is this same "more", however, that sometimes, in his later symbolic paintings, played him false when he surrendered himself wholly to the vision which the spirit of the age inspired in him and which was destined in advance to become a monumental picture. Then that inward inspiration would intentionally be given a spiritual content, breaking through visible reality and entering the realm of the transcendental (pp. 47, 48, 49).

In itself such a picture need not be objectionable, provided one does not become aware of the effort of the artist to tear himself away from reality in order to portray an ecstatic vision. Occasionally Kokoschka was successful in achieving this symbolic painting—for instance, in "The Tempest" (p. 26), a canvas of turbulent emotionality, in which he has portrayed a vision without being impeded by earthly forces.

This painting, done in 1914, of a man and a woman in a boat, who are being driven over the ocean by the irresistible force of a violent storm, vigorously painted in colours dominated by blues and greys, is the image of a complete surrender. Imagination and reality combine to form a synthesis instead of working in opposition, as was often the case with the expressionists. The clash between reality and vision forced Kokoschka to seek a compromise, which he found in the symbol as a bridge between the two. In the symbol, the real and the unreal merge,

6

the dividing line between vision and reality disappears and the dream image becomes the truth. In this case one can indeed speak of a dream image, for here the painter portrayed his love for Alma Mahler (the widow of the composer), who was his muse for some years.

Conscious symbolism breaks through in his painting again and again, particularly at times when he had been under severe emotional strain and when he considered it his duty to make his art subservient to the proclaiming of his militant humanistic beliefs.

The triumph of Hitler in 1933 and the subsequent Nazification of Austria, which compelled Kokoschka to flee to Prague, with the image imprinted on his mind of a betrayed and burning Vienna, caused him to dedicate his artistic abilities to the struggle against inhumanity. Whilst the conservative democratic press in the countries adjacent to Germany neither perceived the seriousness of the situation nor gave heed to the substantiated reports of brutality and persecution, a solitary painter in the city of his forefathers set himself the task of warning humanity, simply because he believed in human rights and human dignity.

It was about then that Kokoschka began to paint his allegorical pictures. At first he painted views of the city of Prague, and he continued to do so until he was driven out of Czecho-Slovakia by Hitler's invading hordes. He had painted similar landscapes in Dresden and Bordeaux, in Paris and Marseilles, in Madrid and Amsterdam. The threatening political situation constantly increased his perturbation, and his realization became ever stronger that his paintings must be symbolical in order to accomplish their purpose—to express his moral conviction.

The first of his works to be imbued with this symbolical character was the portrait of Tomás G. Masaryk, President of Czecho-Slovakia (p. 47), which Kokoschka painted in 1935-36. The painter's own description of the picture clearly explains his intentions:

"At the President's side I paint Amos Comenius, his figure surrounded by the rays of the setting sun. Like a tablet of the law he holds up his *Orbis Pictus,* on which, instead of laws, the five natural indicators, the organs of the senses, are represented. On the other side Prague—the castle, the old Charles Bridge, the river in which children bathe—is to be seen. By a representation of the burning of Huss in the background the days when prejudices become stronger than all reason, when all sense is perverted into nonsense are warningly evoked. Long is the line of T.G. Masaryk's spiritual ancestors, but the line of those who have fought against the spirit is just as long! I want to make it a historical picture; a picture that can be shown in schools, to teach the children that patriotic tasks as well as personal duties are united in humanism." (*Prager Tagblatt*, 8 September, 1935; from Edith Hoffmann's *Kokoschka: Life and Work,* London: Faber and Faber, 1947, the basic biography of Kokoschka).

Hitler and his henchmen gave Kokoschka no more peace than they gave Czecho-Slovakia, where the Sudeten Germans had been made the instruments of a murderous lust for conquest. In July 1937, Hitler had opened in Munich the exhibition of "degenerate art" and had sealed the fate of all modern artists - a group to which, of course, Kokoschka belonged, with eight of his works exhibited there. His paintings were removed from every German art gallery, and in Vienna the police even cut a portrait of Kokoschka into four pieces.

Kokoschka's reply was to paint one of the largest self-portaits of this century, a portrait that can be compared only to the self-portraits of the aging Rembrandt and of Van Gogh, so completely does it express the tragedy of a human being. "Portrait of a 'Degenerate Artist'" was the title Kokoschka gave to his likeness (p. 19).

On the 30th May, 1938, Hitler signed the secret order called the "Grün Plan", in which he stated his determination to strike down Czecho-Slovakia in the near future. On the 18th September of that year the Western democracies gave the Sudeten territory to Germany because of their fear of an already inevitable war. Chamberlain, now a timorous old man, was frightened and still prepared to believe in Hitler's word. He wanted peace for Western Europe, and so he paid the price of Czecho-Slovakia. In Munich he parleyed with Hitler, and when he arrived back at the airport in London, he waved a pitiful scrap of paper. "Peace has been preserved," cried the poor,

Oskar Kokoschka

credulous fellow. On the 1st October, the day Hitler had decided upon long before, the German army marched into Czecho-Slovakia. Kokoschka fled to London, with hardly any money or baggage, wearing one suit, with another in his suitcase, and carrying with him an unfinished painting later to be entitled "Summer" and now hanging in the National Gallery of Scotland, in Edinburgh.

When the Arts Council, in the autumn of 1962, held a large retrospective exhibition of Kokoschka's works in the Tate Gallery in London, the throngs of visitors were so great that they were only equalled by those who had come to the exhibitions of Van Gogh and Picasso. But when Kokoschka came to England in 1938, his name was known only to a small circle in London—though for more than two decades his works had been regarded on the Continent as pinnacles of expressionism, which in his case had acquired a very personal quality. (London had always concentrated more upon Paris than upon the artistic life of Central Europe.)

Very soon a protective and admiring circle formed about him, which, however, could not completely remove from the artist the feeling of being a displaced person. In 1913 Paul Stefan, in his introduction to Kokoschka's *Dramen und Bilder* (Plays and Pictures), had already described Kokoschka as a European; the artist was then only 27, an early age to have gained such a great reputation.

In 1938, when he escaped from the Gestapo, on whose list his name appeared for execution without trial, he was 52. In the years between, he had indeed become a European by virtue of his uninterrupted travels, which took him to Germany, Switzerland, Italy, France, Spain, Portugal, the Netherlands, England, North Africa, Egypt, Turkey and Palestine. He knew no frontiers, either in his travels or in his thoughts, which were founded on the doctrines of the Czech humanist and pacifist Jan Amos Comenius, who in the seventeenth century had been doomed to flee from country to country until he found his final resting place in Amsterdam.

As a refugee in England, Kokoschka felt himself a foreigner, under some kind of restraint and, as the fear of invasion increased amongst the English people, even hunted and threatened with internment. He left London for Polperro in Cornwall, where he felt less anxious and was able to paint again. Here he painted that majestic picture "The Crab" (p. 69), in which that animal is portrayed as a symbol of bestial menace.

But even there he was overtaken by the fearful sensation of being at the mercy of unknown forces, which had caused his former friends, refugees like himself, to be put into internment camps and cut off from the outside world. In the spring of 1940 he returned to London, with his ever faithful and devoted Czech wife Olda, who had fled with him from Prague in 1938. Kokoschka wanted to go underground in the labyrinth of the immense city. "Here, among so many people, they cannot hurt me!" he said (according to Hoffmann).

In the years that followed, Kokoschka wrote a great deal as a fighter for humanist principles, and in some of his paintings we discover the propagandist, the man who expressed his ideas in symbols, in political allegories, for whom even landscapes served his purpose. In his painting of the monstrous crab, which lurks on the beach, lying in wait for the swimmer, who can be recognized as Kokoschka himself (p. 69), the feeling of his involvement in world events is very strong.

In "The Red Egg" (1940-41) Kokoschka flung himself wholeheartedly into the field of political allegory, depicting the sacrificing of Czecho-Slovakia by Hitler, Mussolini, England (the lion) and France (the cat).

After that, in 1942, came "Alice in Wonderland" (p. 70), which was later called "Anschluss" to emphasize that Alice represents Austria. Alice is a naked, innocent little girl who tells the truth, for which reason she stands behind barbed wire. Three air-raid wardens and a frightened woman with a baby, who is wearing a gas-mask, illustrate the "Blitz", as a result of which the buildings in the background are burning.

The series of allegories was continued with "Lorelei" (1942) and "What We Are Fighting For" (1943), the latter especially painted for the "Flight of Freedom" Exhibition of the Artists' International Association in London. This picture reflects the situation in the countries occupied by Hitler. In the foreground lies a woman dead of starvation; her left hand rests on the head

11

of a child that has stretched itself out upon her body. In the centre hangs a crucified Jew, and to his right is a rickshaw, round which stand several figures who are jointly responsible for the misery depicted. To the left stands a machine that produces bones.

When the war was over, Kokoschka put down his thoughts in a pamphlet of many pages entitled "A Petition from a Foreign Artist tot the Righteous People of Great Britain for a Secure and Present Peace". It was signed by him in December 1945, only seven months after the fall of Hitler's Germany, and at that very time Kokoschka declared: "During the war the idea of democracy gave new hope to the despairing world. Today it must be frankly admitted that it does not."

He warns against spiritual uniformity; against supernationalism; against the domination of technique and the industrialization that goes with it, which gives the human being no opportunity to adapt himself spiritually; against everything that threatens the human being as a human being—that is to say, as a soul.

Never before has a painter spoken out so fiercely and so wholeheartedly as Oskar Kokoschka in his "Petition". Nor has a painter ever before argued so earnestly and felt himself so concerned with his fellow human beings, with their simple happiness and their simple life—human beings who seem always to be dependent upon intangible figures who can be recognized only by the loads of orders of knighthood they have collected from here, there and everywhere during years of very varied faithful service.

Whilst the optimistic expectations of a new world after the war gave place everywhere to a reaction of intense distrust, not only among the young people but also among the artists, Kokoschka continued to paint. In 1950 the triptych of "The Prometheus Saga" (p. 48) was completed, in which Kokoschka portrays the tragedy of the human being who threatens to overstep the bounds of that law which has been imposed upon him by his own nature.

In 1954 he painted the triptych "Thermopylae" (p. 49), the main theme of which is the struggle of the Greeks against the Persians 480 years before Christ, but whose spiritual content

12

relates to the period when Kokoschka created the work. Once again he shows himself as the cautionary artist, who uses the allegory of a hopeless struggle fought many centuries ago by a small group of defenders under the command of Leonidas against the huge army of the Persian ruler Xerxes, a struggle in which the Greeks are depicted as the defenders of the people of Europe.

Two years later Kokoschka wrote in the *Schweizer Monatsheft* an essay entitled "The Eye of Darius" in which he describes his encounter with the painting "The Battle between Alexander and Darius" by the sixteenth-century artist Albrecht Altdorfer. This essay not only raises the question "What is reality? Where does it begin and how is it limited?" but also reaches the conclusion: "I would describe 'The Battle between Alexander and Darius' as a work of absolute art."

Kokoschka also sought, with his allegories, to attain the absolute, timeless art of painting. What he says about the work of Altdorfer is just as valid for his own symbolic paintings: "In this work something struggles to be expressed just as in a fugue, but it is fed by an absolute perception and opens up new realms of reality...."

Kokoschka's symbolic and allegorical pictures are not the climax of his total *oeuvre*, though they are the ones to which he feels most attached, because in them, more than in his portraits and his landscapes, he has proclaimed himself a prophet, closely involved with the course of events of his time. One could almost say that all his life he had been painting with the one aim of finally producing such monumental works as "Prometheus" and "Thermopylae" and of thus bearing witness to his concern for the whole human family, which every now and again, alas, forgets its humanity.

This may sound very idealistic, but in Kokoschka's long life so many elements have been combined—his insight into the characters of the subjects of his early portraits, the function of the landscape, his exceptional sense of the dramatic and even of the pathetic, his devotion in both the spoken and the written word to a humanistic society—that the idealism of this serious-minded artist cannot be founded upon other than the basic human values. An artistic career extending over more than sixty years has produced a man of strong emotions and fierce reactions, in whom the rare combination of individualism and social conscience is to be found. In our contemporary world of art this is something to be marvelled at, the more so because symbolism is practically outlawed.

To understand the basic values of Kokoschka's art, we must go back to the Vienna of the turn of the century. In 1905 Kokoschka became a pupil of the School of Arts and Crafts in Vienna. (He was born on the 1st March, 1886, in Pöchlarn on the Danube, the son of a Czech goldsmith. His father had come from Prague to Austria to make a living, which he had lost in his native city because of the bankruptcy of the State. He had married a woman from mountainous Styria, of whom it was said that, like her mother, she possessed the gift of "second sight".)

Vienna from 1905 to 1909 (the year Kokoschka left the School of Arts and Crafts) was a fine gay city, a bulwark of the past, a musical museum, where the performances of Arnold Schönberg's works were received with hisses and whistling. A city supported by the court of Francis Joseph, who in 1908 celebrated the sixtieth year of his reign, and by the dignitaries, the generals and the obsequious, obedient civil servants. A city, too, where a young man—as Max Graf says in his book *The Vienna Opera*—soon lost his conceit and his urge to break new ground, to become a glib, characterless bureaucratic mediocrity.

It is good to know this because the resistance to bureaucratic mediocrity becomes so much more understandable. That is how Vienna became the city where the revolution in modern music began, the so-called twelve-tone system whereby the old laws of tonality were set aside and a new image of sound came into existence. It was in this way that Vienna was to become the city in which Oskar Kokoschka, even as a student at the School of Arts and Crafts, was given unprecedented opportunities.

When, in 1908, the first *Kunstschau* (Art Show) was held in Vienna, an exhibition which created a sensation everywhere, Kokoschka (still a student at the School of Arts and Crafts) came to the fore, not only as a plastic artist with drawings and lithographs, sculpture and decorative panels, but also as a writer, with his drama *Hope of Women* (later titled *Murder*

14

Hope of Women), which he had written the previous year and which was then being performed at the Summer Theatre. This play had been preceded in 1907, on the stage of the School of Arts and Crafts, by his play *Sphinx and Strawman*. These plays were followed by *Schauspiel* (*A Play,* later renamed *The Burning Bush*) in 1911; *Columbus Bound* in 1916; *Job* in 1917; and *Orpheus and Eurydice* in 1918.

It is remarkable how, about 1907-8, when he was some 21 years of age, the young Kokoschka was able to embody expressionistic drama, not only in dramatic content and scenic conception, but also in language, before expressionism had become a renewing stream with such figures as Georg Kaiser, Ernst Toller, Bertold Brecht, Arnolt Bronnen, Fritz von Unruh and Walter Hasenclever.

The revolution that had begun in the plastic arts was carried on in literature. Just as painters, in the first decade of this century, broke away from existing pictorial rules in order to arrive at new forms of expression using new media, so poets also began to occupy themselves with the task of breathing new life into their material.

Being a poet as well as a painter, Kokoschka occupied himself with both these tasks. As a writer of short plays he linked himself not only with a neo-Hellenism which was coming to the fore in literature (Hugo von Hofmannsthal, Rudolf Pannwitz, Paul Ernst), but also with the fervent naturalism of the Swede Strindberg, the Germans Gerhart Hauptmann (in whose works neo-romantic tendencies soon appeared) and Frank Wedekind (who arrived at a symbolical abstraction) and Kokoschka's fellow citizen Arthur Schnitzler, who like Wedekind was possessed by an erotic obsession, not rebellious but resigned and melancholy, which however did not exclude either cynicism or relentless observation on their part.

It was in such an environment as this that Kokoschka created his plays, the themes of which are based upon the relationship between the sexes, with the emphasis more on conflict than on harmony. Elementary passions govern the characters, and their obsessional desires drive them from one violent deed to another. There is always the struggle for mastery between the body and the mind, for the subjection of the woman to the man. But also

15

there is man's struggle against woman, who wants to chain him to the earth and causes him, as well as herself, to die a violent death.

Somebody once said that if Kokoschka had wielded the pen instead of the brush he might well have become the Dostoievski of our century. It was no more than a prophetic surmise, expressed as a token of admiration, but it contained a truth which goes far beyond the plays he wrote between 1907 and 1918; a truth we can discern in his painting, which is based just as much upon conflict and contrast, on the constant struggle of the artist to free himself from earthly bondage and to flee to a purely spiritual domain.

1908. In Paris, quarrels between the admirers of Picasso's cubism and Matisse's fauvism. Picasso was then 27 and Matisse 39. Picasso had just completed two years of work inspired by Negro sculpture and was painting still lifes in which the principle of Cézanne's sphere, cone and cylinder was quite literally interpreted and which in 1909 led both Picasso and Braque to the early cubism: facet-cubism. Portraits and landscapes were represented by geometrical planes, with separation of the planes accomplished by working in depth. French expressionism flourished in the large two-dimensional compositions of Matisse, with their richness of colour against colour and their captivating linear arabesques. André Derain and Maurice de Vlaminck—inspired by Matisse, Gauguin and Van Gogh—were painting fierce landscapes, really quite un-French in feeling.

In Germany the signs of artistic renascence were just as striking. There, also, painters were leaving reality behind in order to achieve a new form of representation. This was not only aesthetically revolutionary, but was based upon a new vision of man, emanating on the one hand from the discovery by Freud of the inner life and on the other hand from a militant social consciousness, though this latter did not lead to an open indictment of society.

In Dresden, in 1905, a community of artists called *"Die Brücke"* (The Bridge) had been founded by four architectural students who had given up the art of building for the art of painting: Ernst Ludwig Kirchner, Fritz Bleyl, Erich Heckel and Karl

Schmidt-Rotluff. *Die Brücke* had no clearly defined purpose, but it produced new ideas, fierce, spontaneous and aggressive. Emil Nolde joined them, though only for a short time, and also Max Pechtstein and Otto Müller.

The Norwegian artist Edvard Munch, his graphic screams laden with a sense of doom and hostility to conservative morality, exercised just as much influence as did the work of Van Gogh, emanating from a tortured soul, and of Paul Gauguin, who, plunging into an illusion of pure primitive life, sought his salvation in Tahiti. Gauguin produced an art which continues to astonish and delight us but which also demonstrates his conquest of the plane by means of linear ornamental forms, within which colour becomes the expression of the spiritual content.

That is a rough outline of the background of Kokoschka in the year 1908. But there is more to it. Gustav Klimt, that admirable painter, the great exponent of the *Jugendstil* (the German term for *art nouveau,* or "modern art") was then in Vienna. He was at the height of his powers at the turn of the century, and long after that continued to work, not only in painting but also in architecture, in fashion and especially in the industrial arts. Vienna was then one of the most important and aggressive centres, along with Barcelona (where the Picasso of the blue and rose period was spiritually born), London, Berlin, Munich, Darmstadt, Weimar, Brussels and Nancy. The decorative line was regarded as "divine", the unique and supreme representative of the symbol that contained a message which was intended to speak to all humanity but which was actually acceptable only to "the happy few".

The history of the *Jugendstil* is extremely complicated, not only as regards its origin (in English pre-Raphaelitism, of the second half of the nineteenth century) but also as to the blossoming of cosmopolitanism towards the end of the century. Not until our own time have its numerous ramifications become clear, for they go back to such varied personalities as Van Gogh, Gauguin, Seurat and Lautrec and the English artists Ruskin, Rossetti, Burne-Jones and Beardsley.

The *Jugendstil* arose out of a sense of life based, on the one hand, on a new social consciousness and, on the other hand, on an

17

aestheticism far removed from real life, which flourished in baroque and in elegant lines, both ornamental in character.

Social consciousness required that art be given a spiritual content, that it express a view of life, even though it may not be one influenced by a literary, philosophic, scientific or religious viewpoint. The solution was ready at hand: symbolism.

The *Jugendstil* was the starting point for Kokoschka. When he began his art studies in Vienna, Gustav Klimt was the only painter of stature, and it was the spiritual influence of Klimt that inspired the series of lithographs which Kokoschka produced in the last months of 1907 to illustrate his own fairy tale "The Dreaming Youths", which was published in book form in 1908 by the Wiener Werkstätte (p. 39).

For a good two years more he remained a student at the School of Arts and Crafts in Vienna, but his lithographs do not reveal him as a slavish imitator of Klimt. On the contrary, Klimt's somewhat weak and elegantly bizarre lines become in the work of Kokoschka stronger and more pregnant, reminding one more of the woodcuts of Gauguin. Kokoschka's lithographs might even be called wilful, a description which could also be applied to the manner in which, contrary to academic tradition, he gave his own interpretation of the models at the School of Arts and Crafts (p. 38). His aim was not to render an anatomic likeness, but a concise description of the woman or man who stood before him, in the form of a pen sketch. When his book *The Dreaming Youths,* with its *Jugendstil*-like lithographs, appeared, Kokoschka already had a new surprise up his sleeve: the drawings he had made for his play *Murder Hope of Women*. In the illustrations for this grim drama he had completely shaken off the *Jugendstil*. He reached ahead almost thirty years; what Picasso and Braque were to do in 1936–38, Kokoschka did in 1908, rendering simultaneously profile and full face, to represent the obsessional inner struggle between man and woman (p. 40).

This may seem incredible, and the explanation cannot solely be based on technical considerations of volume and spatiality. We should rather look for the explanation in the painter's sense of the dramatic, which is one of the basic qualities of his art. Seeking the most forceful means of expressing the feelings

18

(Continued on page 73)

29

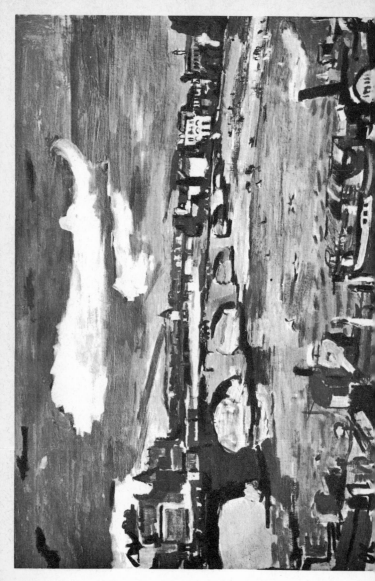

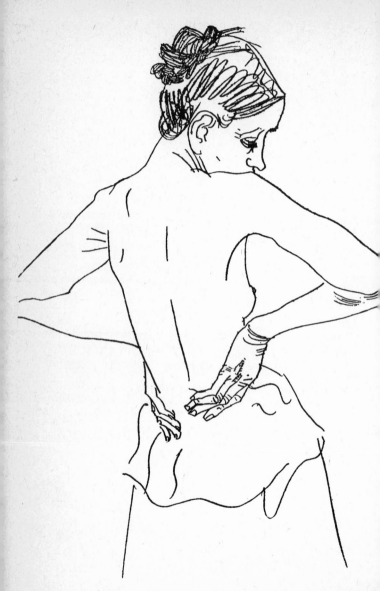

Pradvěst

Muttermila

47

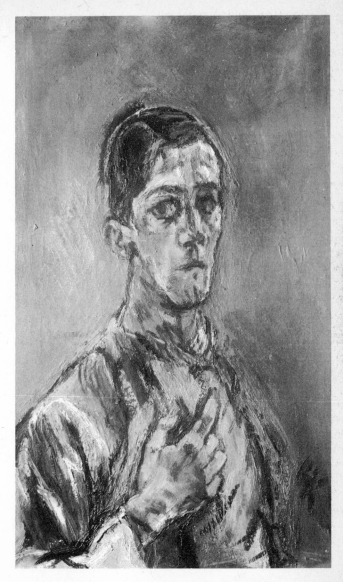

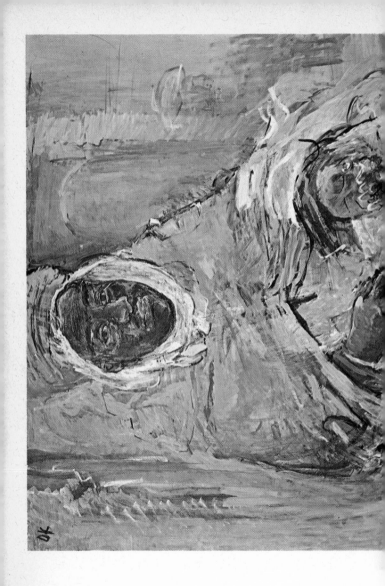

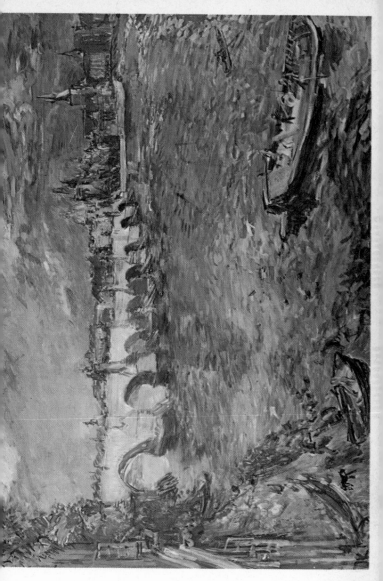

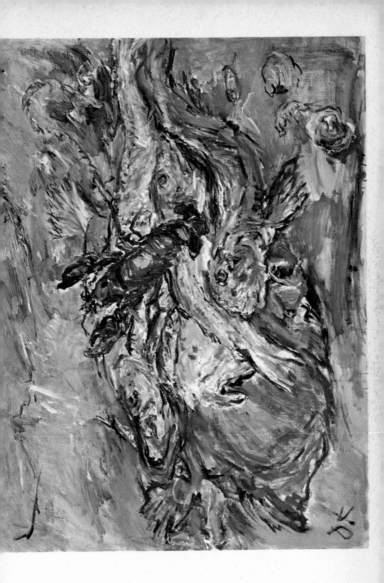

71

underlying his play, he arrived at a spiritually and technically bewildering representation.

The role of the symbol should not, however, be underestimated. The drawings are symbolic, and in that respect Kokoschka not only continued the tradition of the *Jugendstil* but also revealed himself as a painter for whom art is a medium for the expression of dramatic tensions—not for the sake of these tensions in themselves, but for the sake of the human relationships underlying them.

Neither Klimt, Gauguin nor Van Gogh—whose influence is recognizable in Kokoschka's "Still Life with Pine-apple" (1907; p. 20)—determined the course of Kokoschka's development. Just as the revealing fancies of his play *Murder Hope of Women* came from within himself, so it was with his early portraits.

Circumstances too were a compelling factor. Since the 1908 exhibition the Viennese had known the artist as "Wild Kokoschka", a revolutionary, attacked time after time by the bourgeois Viennese press, which could not allow such an obvious opportunity for sensationalism to escape them. As a result Kokoschka was dismissed from his post as assistant instructor at the School of Arts and Crafts, and his scholarship was withdrawn. Long before Hitler had denounced "degenerate artists", that expression had been adopted into the language of the Viennese newspapers as referring to Kokoschka.

The Viennese architect Adolf Loos, himself persecuted by the hyenas of conservatism because he had freed himself from the *Jugendstil* and vehemently opposed all ornamentation which hides the real form, offered Kokoschka a helping hand. He persuaded his friends and acquaintances to give Kokoschka commissions for portraits, and in the latter half of 1909 even arranged for him to go to Switzerland in an effort to enable him to earn his daily bread there by portrait-painting.

His earliest portraits—still in dark colours, mostly greyish—show how fascinated he was by the dramatic quality present in everyone. Each countenance is the embodiment of some hidden or open suffering—anxiety, uncertainty, moral conflict, restlessness or loneliness. Kokoschka ruthlessly portrayed what was contained in the facial structure and expression, so that every portrait became a record of emotions and a certain spiritual state.

For Kokoschka this was still the time for technical experimentation. Every fresh portrait brought new achievements, which were placed in the service of expression. At first the figures were massive, with primitively distinct contours, placed against the background. But soon Kokoschka began to dramatize his sitters. The lines became more angular, the third dimension began to function, the face and hands were strongly modelled and the background itself played a dramatic and structural role.

In the next phase Kokoschka kept his models at a greater distance, and their portrayal was no longer dominated by the earlier more or less psycho-analytic point of view, which the artist realized technically by a laborious and exact application of colour. Now long and powerful brush-strokes emphasize movement and gesture.

In this manner were created a series of the most masterly portraits of our century, masterly in their union of vision and technique. The relentless psychological realism in the fathoming of the character still remains. The painting of the vital essence of his people, of their mental stresses and drives, their obsessions and their life force, is the only thing that counts for the painter, who is guided by a remarkable insight into the spiritual condition of the human being.

Most of his portraits are, of course, pictures of the artistic and intellectual élite of Vienna and Berlin, of people who not only were personalities but who also lived under a creative tension: the progressive architect Adolf Loos (p. 22); the poet Peter Baum (p. 23); the avant-garde publisher Herwarth Walden (p. 24) and many others, like the Viennese writer Karl Kraus (p. 43), the scholar August Forel, the writer Paul Scheerbart and the composers Arnold Schönberg and Anton von Webern. In 1910 Kokoschka went to Berlin. This was the year that Max Pechstein founded *Die neue Sezession* (The New Secession), which organized large exhibitions every year and around which artistic life was centred. Naturally Kokoschka came into close contact with German expressionists. The interest in the art of primitive peoples, which he had already shown as a young artist in Vienna, he found again in Berlin. Here also he was impressed by the rapturous state of living of the Berliners, their passion for life, their urge towards a new community and their aspirations towards new values now that the existing ones had failed.

Nowhere else did the artistic life then possess such *élan* as in Germany. In Munich in 1909 the *Neue Künstlervereinigung* (New Artists' Association) was founded. Then, in 1911, developing out of *Die Brücke* of 1905, the more internationally oriented *Blaue Reiter* (Blue Rider) movement was born in Dresden. The leading figure of this group was the Russian artist Kandinsky, who in 1910 had painted the first absolutely abstract water-colour. Associated with him were Alfred Kubin, Franz Marc, August Macke, Heinrich Campendonk and, a year later, Paul Klee.

At the *Sonderbund* exhibition held in Cologne in 1912, which was an international show of everything new that had appeared in both Germany and France, Kokoschka was represented by six pictures. He was then 26. He had already exhibited in Vienna and Berlin in general and group exhibitions and had had his first one-man show in 1910 at the Galerie Cassirer in Berlin.

Thus he found himself right in the centre of the world of expressionism and was accepted by the expressionists as one of them, but he himself did not feel that he was an expressionist. Kokoschka's objection to the label of "expressionism" on his work is a little difficult to understand. It makes sense, however, if one understands by "expressionism" the typically Germanic, or Northern, school of art, which saw the human being as the central point in the cosmos, with power emanating from him and penetrating to the inner nature of things.

The genuine expressionist was an ecstatic individual, who felt himself allied to the powers of nature and to the universe. He exceeded all bounds in his desires and in his metaphysical conceptions. Expressionism, as the poet Marsman put it, was "a fierce, wild, literally heart-rending cry for the salvation of humanity and the world", a cry born of the inner menace to man of mechanization and capitalism.

Kokoschka's work had little to do with this expressionism, which, incidentally, was to have a short life, and in the early twenties had already entered a spiritual crisis. Naturally, the expressionistic attitude towards life had acted as a stimulant for him and had created a climate in which he could attain self-expression, but at the same time he went far beyond the restricted scope of expressionism and created an art not tied to the spirit of a particular era.

The intoxication characteristic of expressionism is not to be found in Kokoschka's work, nor the linking of art with the striving for new social values. No matter how much Kokoschka was emotionally involved in the events of the time, in his work he always kept the pure art of the painter (portraits and landscapes) quite separate from the humanistic-political preoccupations out of which his symbolical pictures sprang, though — and this is beyond question — the sum total of his work is the expression of an extremely well balanced mind.

Kokoschka's work from 1912 onwards is more direct and more spontaneous than that of the preceding period. It seems as though he is more easily able to approach his sitters with a dynamic perception which enables him to work in firm, broad brushstrokes. He gives his emotions free rein, and his work acquires turbulence and at the same time a sureness of modelling which, better than before, realizes the intensity of the vision without stripping the subject bare after the psycho-analytical manner.

His coloration, which so far had been subdued, now began gradually to bloom. This development first appeared in a group of religious scenes painted in 1911 and can be said to have reached an early peak in the "Double Portrait" of Alma Mahler and Kokoschka (1912-13; p. 25) and in the already described picture "The Tempest" (1914; p. 26), in which the same persons are portrayed.

This is the period of his first symbolical paintings, for we must regard as such the biblical pictures, the portraits of Alma Mahler and Kokoschka and the self-portrait "Knight Errant" (1915; p. 46).

In contrast with his later pictures of this character, these paintings are not yet based upon a militant humanitarian feeling, but on a universal religious or personal sentiment (such as his love for Alma Mahler) or on a psychic situation (such as "Knight Errant", in which the painter dramatizes himself).

This is an important point, because in that period the artistry of Kokoschka was not yet being utilized in his later struggle against injustice and his fervent strivings for a more humane world. But the tendency towards symbolism was inherent in him; on the one hand, it can be seen in the dramatization of the model in his early portraits and, on the other hand, it can be explained as a product of the Viennese environment, dominated by the *Jugendstil*, where he grew up as a young artist.

Just as clear, however, is the influence of several painters: of Vincent Van Gogh, even during the years in Vienna; of El Greco later on, in portraits after 1910 and in pictures like "The Tempest" (p. 26) and "Knight Errant" (p. 46); and of Austrian baroque as a whole, particularly Franz Maulbertsch (1724-96), with his *élan,* drama and ecstasy, to be seen in so many frescoes in Austria.

These influences were in part artistic in character, but were, above all, spiritual. Together, they formed an artist whose very nature had given his painting a spiritual content. Not only the early portraits but all the works that followed bear witness to this fact. The importance of Van Gogh for Kokoschka was less in the technique, so sensational in those days, than in the spiritual nature of his work (the placing of art in the service of a burning faith). The same may be said of the influence of El Greco, Maulbertsch and perhaps also Tintoretto, all of whom pointed out the path for the young painter to follow: the power of dramatization developed to the point to ecstasy, and the symbolism which sometimes accompanied it.

Even Kokoschka reached out for the tangible symbol when in 1915 he returned from the First World War wounded (a shot through the head and a bayonet thrust in the lung) and mentally disturbed. He went through a psychic crisis which, in 1918, led him to have a lifelike doll made, to use instead of a model.

Paul Westheim, in the book *Künstlerbekenntnisse* (Artists' Confessions) (Berlin: Propyläen-Verlag, undated), made public the correspondence between Kokoschka and the lady who was to make this extremely realistic female doll. This is one of the most fascinating documents describing a fetishistic obsession for this life-sized doll was intended to be the ideal wife of the painter. Kokoschka wrote:

"As I can bear no living people but am often delivered to despair when alone, I beg you again to use all your imagination, all your sensitiveness for the ghostly companion you are preparing for me and to breathe into her such life that in the end, when you have finished the body, there is no spot which does not radiate feeling, to which you have not applied yourself to overcome by the most complex devices the dead material; then will all the delicate and intimate gifts of nature displayed in the female body be recalled to me in some desperate hour by some symbolic hieroglyph, or sign, with which you have secretly endowed that bundle of rags." (From Edith Hoffmann's *Kokoschka: Life and Work,* London: Faber & Faber, 1947.)

Many were the letters that Kokoschka wrote, between the 22nd July, 1918 and the 6th April, 1919 to the maker of this doll, Fräulein M.; he wrote the most meticulous instructions and sent her large, detailed drawings. It stands to reason that this fetish—for as such we must look upon this lifelike doll—which was to have been a being without uncontrolled instincts, without hatred, without any of those traits that make a human being ugly, was a disappointment.

The artist endeavoured to bring this lifeless object to life in his picture "Woman in Blue" (p. 28). For this picture, according to Hans Maria Wingler, he made, between April and June, 1919, about 160 preliminary drawings—a testimony to his obsessive desire to create life out of a dead thing. This painting, however, marked the beginning of a fresh period, one in which Kokoschka achieved his greatest creations, with colour triumphant.

When he came back from the First World War, wounded and mentally disordered, Kokoschka covered his canvas in a staccato-like style with irregular, almost formless splotches of paint. There was a certain bold vigour in this method, in several respects reminiscent of Van Gogh, but the crude application of the paint laid on thickly in winding strokes suggests all too much the expression of an unbalanced mind.

Thanks, however, to his obsession with painting the portrait of the doll, Kokoschka arrived at a new phase in which, through the plastic medium of his paint, he built up a structure in which contours were no longer necessary. Now his coloration became warm and rich; brilliant yellows, blues and reds of almost explosive intensity but also, usually, of poetic power, predominate. Out of this period, which continued until about 1923, came masterpieces such as "The Power of Music" (p. 27), the "Double Portrait of Hans Mardersteig and Carl Georg Heise" (pp. 30, 31) and "Two Girls" (p. 29) — though in the last picture the coloration is subdued, as it was increasingly to become in the years ahead. It could hardly have been otherwise, for after having gone to the extreme in his coloration Kokoschka inevitably had to return to more restrained colours. His pictures became more closely attuned to reality, and his fanatical zeal was kept within the bounds of his keen powers of perception.

This quality showed itself sooner in his landscapes than in his portraits. Indeed, his landscapes had always been closer to reality, because in them he was not confronted with states of mind. In fact, he had not been much interested in landscapes before he settled in Dresden in 1917 (in 1919 he became a professor at the Academy there). In 1909, during his first stay in Switzerland, he had painted his "Dent du Midi"; in 1913, "Alpine Landscape at Mürren", "Naples in a Storm" and "Dolomite Landscape, Tre Croci"; in 1916-17, "Landscape in Saxony"; and in 1917, "Stockholm Harbour" (done when he had gone there for treatment of the mental disorder caused by the war).

But these landscapes were, for him, merely incidental works. Kokoschka's landscape painting began to be of some importance in the years when he lived in Dresden, with "Dresden, Neustadt V" (p. 33) and "Dresden, Augustus Bridge with Steamboat II" (p. 32). These are rich, colourful, vigorous paintings, monumental in vision, with powerfully expressive planes. His other works from this period — either portraits (pp. 30, 31) or genre-like pictures such as "Two Girls" (p. 29) and "The Slave Girl" (p. 34) — are marked by a luxuriant baroque and an intense dramatic quality, whilst his views of the Elbe are always striking in their simplicity and harmony.

It was, however, in 1924, when his environment in Dresden had begun to oppress him and he became, in the true sense of the word, a European (because then the years of his many travels began), that he commenced the series of landscapes which have become unique in the history of modern art: 1924: Switzerland, Paris; 1925: France (Bordeaux, Biarritz, Avignon, Marseilles), Monte Carlo, Spain, London, Portugal, Amsterdam; 1926: London, Berlin; 1927: Berlin, Paris, Venice, Switzerland; 1928: Africa; 1929: Paris, Ireland, Scotland, Egypt, Turkey, Palestine, Munich; 1930: Paris, Vienna, Algiers, Italy. From 1931 through 1934 he lived alternately in Vienna and Paris.

From each city Kokoschka carried away with him, on canvas, his own vision, his own image. His paintings are not just views of cities, they are portraits, actual likenesses, such as he had always made of persons. He used the places that served as his models just as he once wrote with regard to his sitters: "to construct compositions illustrating the conflict of man against man, the contrasts between one and another, such as that between hate and love, and in each picture I seek for that dramatic emphasis which gives the individual a higher unity."

Though some of Kokoschka's landscapes, his French ones especially, may have a certain joyousness in their coloration, resulting from a delicate use of the brush, the spirit that had been nourished on Strindberg and Wedekind was not absent in his landscapes. It is this spirit which explains his preference for those landscapes which show the contrast between ancient architecture and modern life and in which there are other elements that create dramatic tension.

Friction, contrast and conflict form the foundation of Kokoschka's work, and this holds good in equal measure for his portrayal of people and landscapes. That is why he humanizes the city, in the sense that on his canvases the city is a real living organism, activated by the ecstasy of the artist :"Marseilles Harbour II" (p. 61); "Amsterdam, Kloveniersburgwal" (p. 62); "London, Tower Bridge" (p. 63); "Biarritz Beach" (p. 64); "London, Large Thames View I" (p. 65); "Jerusalem" (p. 66); "Prague, Charles Bridge with Boat" (p. 67); "Chamonix, Mont Blanc" (p. 68); and, finally, "View of the Thames from the Vickers Building, Millbank" (p. 72). This last picture was painted in 1962 and is quite different from all the other landscapes mentioned above, which date from the 1925 to 1934 period.

The human being, as a figure, rarely plays a part in these land-scapes, and yet the paintings are exceptionally human, because they make one realize that the cities have been created by human beings and are lived in by human beings, people of a definite character, who have imprinted their distinctive stamp upon them. This almost visionary eye of the painter, which at the same time takes in the social life of the cities, gives Ko-koschka's landscapes their meaning, their greatness and their exceptional character. For in these city-portraits of humanitarian and psychological charm, the products of a moving as well as revealing vision and a painterly technique that expressed the spirit of the age, the spirit of the painter himself and the character of the city-portrait, a rare artistic *oeuvre* was created.

Kokoschka has written a great deal about visual consciousness. "The state of awareness of visions is not one in which we are either remembering or perceiving. It is rather a level of con-sciousness at which we experience visions within ourselves. . . . Yet the awareness of such imagery is a part of living. It is life selecting from the forms which flow towards it or retraining at will," wrote Kokoschka in 1912 in "On the Nature of Visions" (translated by Hedi Medlinger and John Thwaites; from Edith Hoffmann's *Kokoschka: Life and Work*).

Thirty-five years later, in 1947, he had not yet exhausted his theories on the nature of vision. In "Image, Speech and Writing" he remarks: "Vision is a gift for which human beings of certain circles of culture have to thank their con-sciousness. In visual consciousness a conception of form finds expression which permits a human world with its own laws to emerge out of the stream of events. . . . We must not forget that 'visual consciousness' signifies a state of mind which gives, us an insight into the world of appearances and a sense of community. In this way a world-view is created which is naturally bound up with the period."

In 1953, when Kokoschka was 67 and he commenced to lecture at the International Summer School for the Visual Arts in Salzburg, his course was called "The School of Vision".

In 1947 he had become a British subject, and his new country later conferred a high royal decoration upon him, after the West German Bundestag had awarded him their Order of

Merit on the occasion of his seventieth birthday, in 1956. As a European, he has lived, since 1953, at Villeneuve, Switzerland, on Lake Geneva, his base for numerous journeys to London, Austria, Greece, Italy, America, Sicily, Rome, Paris, Hamburg and a host of other countries and cities.

Kokoschka still receives a flood of commissions, mostly for portraits, and the only defence the aged painter puts up is: "But I like painting." Since 1945 many studies of his work have been published, among which those of Hans Maria Wingler and Edith Hoffman must be mentioned. Exhibitions have followed one after the other in ever-increasing glory: the Biennial at Venice in 1947; in the same year, an exhibition that travelled a whole year through America; in 1956, at Prague and Salzburg; in 1958, at Munich, Vienna and The Hague; in 1960, at Copenhagen and London; and, in 1962, at London and Hamburg.

And in contrast to all this glory, there stands one portrait, an unforgettable likeness of Kokoschka himself, his "Portrait of a 'Degenerate Artist' ", painted in 1937 in Prague, when all his works (147 of them) in the German art galleries were confiscated by the Nazis. It is one of the many self-portraits (pp. 19, 50-54) that he has made in the course of the years. With broad, impassioned and defiant brush-strokes the artist painted his own likeness at a moment when not only was the significance of his work unrecognized, but the work itself was condemned.

One has only to compare this portrait with those of the composer Arnold Schönberg (p. 35), of Nancy Cunard (p. 36), of the poet Ernst Blass (p. 55) or of Adele Astaire (p. 57) to appreciate the almost frightening intensity with which this self-portrait was painted. Of course, a good ten years lie between the other portraits and the "Portrait of a 'Degenerate Artist' " during which Kokoschka's style had acquired a fiercer wielding of the brush and a coloration which constantly spoke a more powerful language, as was also the case with his landscapes and his later symbolical paintings, but with such a likeness as this self-portrait years hardly count.

In that painting the past and the future are reflected: the painter of the unprecedentedly realistic portraits of the years before the First World War and the painter of the symbolical pictures which began in Prague and continued until after the Second World War. It is, as it were, the opposite pole to one of his finest animal paintings, "The Mandrill" (1926; p. 59).

If this portrait of the ape was the embodiment of elementary passion, then the "Portrait of a 'Degenerate Artist' " was the symbol of man's unyielding resistance to the beast who had been given the opportunity, with his brown and black hordes, to bring death and destruction to a large part of the world.

It is a proud and defiant portrait, the portrait of a resistance fighter, painted before that phrase had any meaning in the countries of Europe. It is the portrait of a man who was appalled by what he saw happening and by what he foresaw; a man who believed in the redemption of mankind through education and had always been opposed to tyranny and war, against politicians and their egocentric and often blind policies.

Kokoschka's eye and his mind have always been searching, perhaps mercilessly at times. The human being that he was as a painter has made him one of the very great men of our century. Kokoschka was a revolutionary, both as man and artist— though in both respects he was also allied with tradition—a builder of the future and a renewer in the world of painting and also in the world of the human spirit.

LIST OF ILLUSTRATIONS

25 DOUBLE PORTRAIT (OSKAR KOKOSCHKA AND ALMA MAHLER)
1912-13; oil; 39⅝×35½ in.;
collection of Professor Edgar Horstmann, Hamburg

26 THE TEMPEST
1914; oil; 71¼×86⅝ in.; Kunstmuseum, Basle
The figures represent Alma Mahler and Oskar Kokoschka,
who are drifting over the ocean in a small boat. The
painting could be described as a love poem.

27 THE POWER OF MUSIC
1919; oil; 40⅛×59 in.;
Stedelijk van Abbemuseum, Eindhoven, Holland

28 WOMAN IN BLUE
1919; oil; 29½×39⅜ in.;
Württembergische Staatsgalerie, Stuttgart
The painting of the life-sized doll which Kokoschka had
made for him (see pp. 77-78).

29 TWO GIRLS
About 1921; oil; 46×31½ in.;
collection of Mrs. Frederick Knize, New York

30 DOUBLE PORTRAIT OF HANS MARDERSTEIG AND
31 CARL GEORG HEISE
1919; oil; in two parts, each part 39⅜×28⅜ in.;
Museum Boymans-van Beuningen, Rotterdam
Originally both portraits were painted on one canvas, which
was later cut into two parts. Mardersteig and Heise were
editors of the review *Genius,* to which Kokoschka con-
tributed.

32 DRESDEN, AUGUSTUS BRIDGE WITH STEAMBOAT II
1923; oil; 25⅝×37⅜ in.;
Stedelijk van Abbemuseum, Eindhoven, Holland

33 DRESDEN, NEUSTADT V
1922-23; oil; 27¼×42½ in.;
collection of Mr. Sam Spiegel, New York

34 THE SLAVE GIRL
1923-24; oil; $43\frac{1}{4} \times 31\frac{1}{2}$ in.; collection of Mr. and Mrs. Morton D. May, St. Louis, U.S.A.

35 PORTRAIT OF THE COMPOSER ARNOLD SCHÖNBERG
1924; oil; $39 \times 29\frac{1}{2}$ in.;
collection of Mrs. Frederick Knize, New York

36 PORTRAIT OF NANCY CUNARD
1924; oil; $45\frac{5}{8} \times 28\frac{3}{4}$ in.;
collection of Dr. Bernhard Sprengel, Hanover, Germany

37 THE LADY'S MAID
1925; oil; 30×22 in.;
collection of Dr. Max Fischer, Stuttgart

38 THE ACROBAT'S DAUGHTER
About 1908; pencil drawing; $17\frac{7}{8} \times 13\frac{1}{2}$ in.;
Collection of Anton Walbrook, London

39 THE DREAMING YOUTHS: THE GIRL LI AND I
1908; lithograph; $9\frac{3}{4} \times 8\frac{1}{2}$ in.;
Graphische Sammlung, Staatsgalerie, Stuttgart
One of eight coloured lithographs which Kokoschka made to illustrate his own book *The Dreaming Youths,* published in Vienna in 1908 by the Wiener Werkstätte.

40 MURDER HOPE OF WOMEN
1908; pen and brush drawing in India ink; $8\frac{1}{2} \times 6\frac{7}{8}$ in.;
Graphische Sammlung, Staatsgalerie, Stuttgart
One of four drawings Kokoschka made for his play *Murder Hope of Women,* first published with the text of the play in the Berlin review *Der Sturm* in 1910.

41 PIETÀ (THE HUMAN TRAGEDY)
1908; lithograph; $48 \times 31\frac{1}{4}$ in.;
Austrian Museum of Applied Art, Vienna
Poster for the Summer Theatre, Vienna, Art Show, 1908

42 PORTRAIT OF YVETTE GUILBERT
1910; one of 20 drawings which, after publication in the *Der Sturm* in 1913, were issued in a folder by *Der Sturm*.

43 PORTRAIT OF KARL KRAUS

1910; one of 15 drawings of friends and collaborators of the review *Der Sturm*, published by *Der Sturm* in an album called "Human Heads" in 1916.

44 COLUMBUS BOUND: PORTRAIT OF A WOMAN IN PROFILE TO THE RIGHT

1913; lithograph; $8\frac{3}{4} \times 7\frac{1}{2}$ in.; one of twelve lithographs made by Kokoschka for his dramatic poem *Columbus Bound*; the complete series was published in 1916 by Kurt Wolff in Berlin; a smaller edition was issued in 1921 by Fritz Gurlitt in Berlin.

45 O EWIGKEIT—DU DONNERWORT (Oh Eternity—Thou Fearful Word) (Bach Cantata): "*Wohlan soll ich von nun an selig sein* (I shall be in bliss from now on)"

1914; lithograph; $17\frac{3}{4} \times 13\frac{3}{8}$ in.; one of nine lithographs published by Fritz Gurlitt in Berlin in album form in 1916-17.

46 KNIGHT ERRANT

1915; oil; $35\frac{1}{2} \times 71$ in.;
The Solomon R. Guggenheim Museum, New York

47 TOMÁS G. MASARYK, President of Czecho-Slovakia

1935-36; oil; $38\frac{5}{8} \times 51\frac{1}{4}$ in.;
Carnegie Institute (Patrons' Art Fund), Pittsburgh

48 THE PROMETHEUS SAGA: APOCALYPSE

1950; tempera; centre panel of triptych; $90\frac{1}{2} \times 138$ in.;
collection of Count Antoine Seilern, London

49 THERMOPYLAE: THE BATTLE

1954; tempera; centre panel of triptych; $88\frac{1}{2} \times 118$ in.;
Hochschulabteilung, Schulbehörde, Hamburg

50 SELF-PORTRAIT WITH CAP

1932; oil; $38\frac{5}{8} \times 28$ in.;
private collection, England

51 SELF-PORTRAIT WITH CROSSED ARMS

1923; oil; $43\frac{1}{4} \times 27\frac{1}{2}$ in.; private collection, Germany

52 SELF-PORTRAIT
1917; oil; 30¾×24⅜ in.; von der Heydt Museum of Wuppertal, Wuppertal-Elberfeld, Germany

53 SELF-PORTRAIT
About 1913; oil; 31⅞×19¾ in.;
Museum of Modern Art, New York

54 THE PAINTER AND HIS MODEL II
1924; oil; 33⅛×50¾ in.; collection of Mr. and Mrs. Morton D. May, St. Louis, U.S.A.

55 PORTRAIT OF ERNST BLASS
1925; oil; 31½×47¼ in.;
Kunsthalle, Bremen

56 NUDE IN LANDSCAPE NEAR AVIGNON
1925; oil; 15×17¾ in.; collection of the late Dr. W. R. Valentiner, Raleigh, North Carolina, U.S.A.

57 PORTRAIT OF ADELE ASTAIRE
1926; oil; 37¾×51½ in.; Kunsthaus, Zurich
Adele Astaire, sister of the dancer and film actor Fred Astaire, married Lord Charles Cavendish.

58 HINDS
1926; oil; 51¼×35 in.; private collection

59 THE MANDRILL
1926; oil; 50×39¾ in.;
Museum Boymans-van Beuningen, Rotterdam

60 THE MARABOUT OF TEMACINE
1928; oil; 38¼×51¼ in.;
collection of Professor Edgar Horstmann, Hamburg

61 MARSEILLES HARBOUR II
1925; oil; 28¾×39⅜ in.;
City Art Museum, St. Louis, U.S.A.

62 AMSTERDAM, KLOVENIERSBURGWAL
1925; oil; 24½×33½ in.;
Städtische Kunsthalle, Mannheim, Germany
Painted from the Hotel Doelen.

63 LONDON, TOWER BRIDGE
1925; oil; 30×50⅜ in.;
Institute of Art, Minneapolis, U.S.A.

64 BIARRITZ BEACH
1925; oil; 29⅛×43¼ in.; Fogg Art Museum, Harvard
University, Cambridge, Mass., U.S.A.

65 LONDON, LARGE THAMES VIEW I
1926; oil; 35½×51¼ in.;
Albright-Knox Art Gallery, Buffalo, N.Y., U.S.A.

66 JERUSALEM
1929; oil; 31½×50¾ in.;
Detroit Institute of Arts, Detroit, U.S.A.

67 PRAGUE, CHARLES BRIDGE WITH BOAT
1934; oil; 33½×47⅝ in.; National Museum, Prague

68 CHAMONIX, MONT BLANC
1927; oil; 35½×51¼ in.; Kunsthalle, Karlsruhe

69 THE CRAB
1939-40; oil; 24¾×30 in.; collection of Sir Edward and
Lady Beddington-Behrens, London

70 ALICE IN WONDERLAND ("ANSCHLUSS")
1942; oil; 24¾×30 in.; private collection, Switzerland
A political allegory of the *Anschluss* (annexation) of Austria
in 1938; an indictment of Hitler's militarism.

71 FLOOD IN HAMBURG
1962; oil; 35½×46½ in.;
Marlborough Fine Art Ltd, London
Kokoschka intended to paint a still life in the Fish Market
when the city was suddenly flooded as the result of a storm.
He then painted this picture.

72 VIEW OF THE THAMES FROM THE VICKERS BUILDING, MILL-
BANK (detail)
1962; oil; 36×50 in.;
Marlborough Fine Art Ltd, London